Reflections

KELVIN
CRUICKSHANK

PENGUIN BOOKS

PENGUIN

UK | USA | Canada | Ireland | Australia
India | New Zealand | South Africa | China

Penguin is an imprint of the Penguin Random House group of companies,
whose addresses can be found at global.penguinrandomhouse.com.

Penguin
Random House
New Zealand

First published by Penguin Random House New Zealand, 2018

10 9 8 7 6 5 4 3 2 1

Design by Cat Taylor © Penguin Random House New Zealand
Cover photograph of Kelvin © Becky Nunes
Background imagery by Roman Sakhno, 85819045/Shutterstock
Prepress by Image Centre Group
Printed and bound in Australia by Griffin Press, an Accredited
ISO AS/NZS 14001 Environmental Management Systems Printer

A catalogue record for this book is available from
the National Library of New Zealand.

ISBN 978-0-14-377230-9
eISBN 978-0-14-377231-6

penguin.co.nz

To everyone who has experienced loss, this book is for you. Through acceptance we can let the past go and retrain ourselves with positive reinforcements to allow joy and happiness back into our lives. May you find inner peace and freedom.

Listen up

THERE COMES A TIME IN each of our lives when we must look deep inside ourselves. To succeed on this Earth, we need to know who we really are. We must come to understand our strengths and weaknesses, our passions and dreams, and what really makes us tick. I believe this collection of some of my innermost thoughts and advice will help with that. I certainly don't think of these words of wisdom as coming directly from me – instead, they are the result of a lifetime of communicating with spirit. Those who have crossed over have so much knowledge to pass on to those of us who are willing to listen up.

Within these pages are 365 thoughts to help you on your journey through life – a quote a day for a year. Whether you read one each day or simply take inspiration when you need it by opening up to a random page, I hope these words will bring you motivation and comfort. You might wake up each morning and take a look at that day's thought to give you direction for the day ahead, or you could spend time reading through a few pages when – for whatever reason – you are feeling down. However you choose to use this book, I hope you will think of it as a trusted friend you can call on at any time for guidance.

In times of grief, it's easy to forget that our loved ones in spirit only want what's best for us. They certainly don't want us to wallow in sadness! Next time you feel dragged down by the weight of your sorrow, try to think of this and remember that whoever you lost would want you to be happy and to get on with life. Here's the amazing thing: your loved ones in Heaven are still able to be with you, just not in the same form as they were on Earth. If you think of them, they will be drawn to you. They will see what you are doing, hear what you are saying, and they can communicate with you if you are open to it. Isn't that incredible?

Whenever you are feeling overwhelmed, take a moment to kick back with a cup of tea and delve into this book. I know what you're thinking – 'But, Kelvin, I'm too busy to find the time to do that!'

Trust me, it's when you're busiest that you most need to take a step back and gain a bit of perspective on what is important and what can wait a day or two. Can that load of washing be left until tomorrow? Is your boss going to mind if you ask for an extra hour to complete that report? Will your partner step up and take the kids to Saturday sports so you can have a lie-in? Ask for help and understanding from those around you – it might surprise you to see how happy they are to give you a break.

We all have days where we need a bit of a boost – a reminder that our time on this Earth is precious, so we should make the most of every moment. I hope this book will provide that support whenever you need it most.

With love,
Kelvin

Thoughts and affirmations for every day of the year

Begin each year afresh, with new hopes and aspirations for the time ahead. Set aside some time on the first day of January to note down all that you wish to achieve in the coming months, and then hold yourself accountable to it. Dream it, and you can achieve it.

One day at a time – keeping it real – is so important. Before coming to this earthly experience, you sat with the Creator and had a conversation about what to do while you were here to grow and to learn. Have faith knowing that you have chosen well.

Dreams are a dress rehearsal for life, where your spirit or your inner self shows you what's really going on. If you had a dream about running away from something negative and weren't aware of the role dreams play, you'd just think you had a really crazy dream. But if you are aware of their importance, you can decide to take control of that dream – ask yourself what it means, and stand up and face your fears. It signifies you are probably running from something in reality, and standing up to it can change your whole life.

Learn to stand your ground, and be strong. Nobody likes going through negative experiences, but they make you who you are. Spiritually, they offer a huge learning curve.

Life comes down to experiences. When you're born you don't know who you are. As soon as you're born you forget where you came from, and where you've been. Your job initially is to understand who you are. Understanding brings release. We are here to remember where we have been, and to complete the jigsaw of life.

～

You don't need to be educated to be successful; you just need to follow your dreams.

～

Be true to yourself and trust your instincts as to what makes your heart sing. Always follow your passions.

Grief can be overwhelming. It can make you bitter, twisted and angry. It can make you so sad you are not sure how you are going to get up in the morning and make it through the day. It can bog you down and hold you back until you are no longer living life. It can break your heart into thousands of tiny pieces. But being like this is no way to live. Please believe me when I say that your loved one who has crossed over does not want to see you like this. They miss you, too, but they want to see you getting on with your life. They want you to leave behind the anguish, the sadness, the hurt and the anger, and enjoy yourself again. Life is for living – make the most of it!

Affirmations and prayer are powerful tools. It doesn't matter what affirmations you use, as long as it makes you feel good. If you can recite the whole affirmation without a break, you're sweet. If you're reciting an affirmation but your concentration is broken and you start thinking about whatever's going on at work, or you start going off into la la land, then that negative vibration is still with you. You must recite, recite – and if you get cut off, start over. When you can repeat it, one time after the other, that clears that negative vibration from you.

If you are getting signs that things aren't right, listen to them. Trust your instincts.

When you get home after a hard day, visualise all your problems on your clothes. When you get changed, throw the problems in the washing basket along with the clothing. Let it all go.

⁓

I have experienced Heaven, and it was overwhelming. The feelings in that environment were unconditional love to the fullest: no pressure, no judgment, no hatred, no anger, no violence – nothing but safety. Complete safety. Protected, nurtured, humble, compassionate. This is what your loved ones who have crossed are experiencing.

Be strong. The lessons you have chosen for this life may be long and hard, but you will make it through and the outcome could be beyond your wildest dreams. And those dear to you who have crossed over will always be at your side to help.

Many people live in fear of death – their own and that of loved ones – but there is nothing to be afraid of. Heaven is an incredible place.

Try to understand that everything happens for a reason, whether we get it right away or have to wait for answers. Things do work out.

We are only here once in this body, so we should make the most of it. However, I also absolutely believe that we can come back for more experiences, good or bad, if we need to for our spiritual learning.

Trust what the Creator and spirit have lined up for you. Trust their guidance as new life experiences come to hand.

There are lots of different factors in how you choose to live. Personally, I think we just need to get off the sofa! Get off it and get out there – live your dreams.

Stay honest and true, and be at peace with yourself and everything in life. You might stuff up now and again – we all do – but pick yourself up and keep going.

Be the best version of yourself. In your lifetime you will make mistakes, but don't let this stop you from always trying to better yourself. Imagine how great the world would be if we all did that!

Worrying about things you can't change solves nothing. You can only control your own actions, so concentrate on that instead of what you cannot change.

Shut off your cellphone, TV and computer
every now and again. Disconnecting once in
a while is good for the soul.

To walk in light is to be at peace with
everything in life, to accept that everything
happens for a reason, even if we can't at first
understand what that reason is. To walk
in light is to accept who you are, and to be
honest and true.

I truly believe life's what we make it. I reckon
we should go with the flow, trusting each day
as it comes along.

Many of my interactions with spirit contain universal insights into the most fundamental questions of our earthly life – forgiveness, spirituality, faith, life, death and the nature of love. The loss of a friend or a family member brings all of these questions right to the fore. Dealing with loss is a massive challenge, but your loved ones in Heaven have only messages of love and reassurance.

Let go of your grief for your loved ones. Honour their memory, and remember the happy times you shared, but be sure to move on with your own life as well.

We all have to go through traumatic experiences. As hard as these experiences are at the time, you must understand that they are an important part of your learning.

Spirituality is not about organised religion – although many people obviously find that established religions are the best place for them to practise their spirituality – but is essentially a personal matter. Look inside yourself to find your own spirituality.

Understand that what will be will be. Instead of trying to fight fate and make your life what everybody thinks it should be, just relax and do what you feel is right.

Never lose faith. There's no doubt about it, you will go through testing times in your lifetime, but ultimately the universe will look after you.

The power of emotions and of love between people can be so strong that it can create a bridge between this world and the spirit world. Being assured of the continuing love of spirit really can change your life.

∽

When we feel loved, we feel validated, we feel whole. Remember to tell your family every day how much you love them.

Much of my work is carried out with people enduring the most difficult times of their life: loss of loved ones, grief, depression, disappointment – even murder. You name it, I see it every day. But despite all that, or more likely because of it, I think it is very important to have some laughs to remind us that life can be good. Humour is good for the soul.

Pat yourself on the back for how far you have come. It's easy to forget all of your achievements and progress, but if you look back over the past few years I'm sure you'll see how much you have to be proud of.

There's no need to be afraid of dying. When we cross over, there's an amazing afterlife waiting for us.

～

You are not alone. It may not always feel like it, but your loved ones in spirit will always be watching over you.

～

You are on this Earth to experience as much as possible. Savour the good times, but don't dwell on the bad – life is short, so make the most of every moment.

Our relatives and friends who are in the afterlife still want what's best for us. Love is endless – not even death can break that bond.

⌒⌒

Indecisiveness will get you nowhere. Don't be afraid to make a decision and stand by your choice – after all, you are doing what you feel is right at the time. Who can ask for more than that?

Just put one foot in front of the other. That's all you need to do for now.

⁓

If you find yourself putting off a tough conversation – be it with your partner, your boss or a friend – visualise yourself getting that talk out of the way and how good you'll feel once it's done.

When a partner, close friend or family member dies, we can be left with a whole mixture of emotions. Grief is complicated, and can be overshadowed by anger or guilt. Release your feelings of hurt and anger, so you can move forward.

Come clean about any secrets you have – you might be surprised by the weight that lifts from your shoulders, and how your relationships are strengthened as a result. In a healthy life there is no space for secrets and unfinished business.

Stay strong. You may be struggling at the moment, but trust me: you won't struggle forever. Good times are ahead.

We carry inside ourselves the bad things other people have said about us – sometimes we take on board those opinions and believe the worst of ourselves. We carry the tag. We have to cut those tags loose, because they belong to somebody else. It's only their opinion.

You are an amazing person, and it's important to spend this lifetime getting to know yourself and appreciating all that makes you who you are. If you make a mistake, instead of being hard on yourself, take it as a lesson and move on. Love every unique inch of yourself.

If a loved one passes after a long illness, we can experience many different emotions. Often there is relief for that person – the knowledge that their suffering is at an end. There can be relief for the family, especially for those who have taken responsibility for caring for the ill person, sometimes for years. But very often, even if you've had all that time to prepare, you're never really prepared at the end of the day for the experience of loss. Often, we begin to worry. We begin to experience regret and guilt. When you handle grief in this way, it will become a burden because you will blame yourself for not doing the right things. Remember you did what was best for the person who was ill, taking into consideration your own limitations, broader responsibilities and constraints.

Heaven's not a faraway place, it's only an arm's length away – and so are all of your loved ones who have crossed over. How wonderful is that?

⌒

Learn how to say no sometimes. People will always want something from you, but you can fit in only so much each day. You're the only one with the ability to truly look out for yourself.

⌒

Love is about being truthful. We need to be able to tell our loved ones the truth about our own lives, so that we can have truly healthy relationships in this life.

It takes courage to acknowledge your fear but to take the risk anyway. There will always be enormous spiritual benefits to you from acting courageously.

Rejection is one of the most devastating emotions we can feel. From being turned down for a job through to being cast aside by a partner because they found someone they like better, rejection is an incredibly painful experience. It leaves us doubting ourselves and our worth, and we can end up thinking, 'Why aren't I good enough?' Well, how you want things to turn out and how they are actually mapped out for you are often two very different things. When things don't work out you can try your hardest to fix them, but if you're not successful you need to accept that you are going against what is written.

Shoot for your dreams, but don't do it in a way that causes harm to others. If you don't behave in an ethical way, or if you are dishonest – particularly to those you love – you fail yourself and let yourself down.

Have a little faith. Know that even though you can't see the path in front of you, everything will turn out fine.

When you gain wisdom from a situation, how can you see that as failure? Take it as a learning curve and move on.

Find the time to get out in the great outdoors. I'm happiest on my boat with a rod in hand, but for you it might be going for a hike or swimming in the ocean. Enjoy all that Mother Nature has to offer.

Do you struggle to cope with change? Just remember that change is a natural, healthy part of progressing in life.

Reduce your stress levels by not committing to more than you can realistically manage.

Take some time to escape the hustle and bustle of your everyday life. A peaceful break – whether it's a trip away or simply a quiet week at home – will do wonders for your soul.

The holiday season can be a lonely time if you have recently lost someone. Be sure to embrace your family and friends, and be open to the support they'll give.

Grief may not completely disappear with time, but the pain does ease and life does go on.

~~~

Procrastination gets you nowhere. We're all guilty of it sometimes, but we need to step up and get things done. Just think how good it feels when you finish a task you have been putting off!

If you feel like someone is judging you, just ignore them. They're entitled to their opinion, but you shouldn't let it affect you.

It's okay to miss someone who has passed. Just don't let your grief hold you back – that person would want you to move forward with your life.

Instead of blaming others for what's gone wrong, look inside yourself to see what you can do to change your life for the better.

⁓

If you find that you've taken on too much, don't feel bad about cutting back some of your commitments. Others will understand that you simply don't have the time, and if they don't, that's their issue to overcome.

⁓

It's okay to cry. Don't bottle up your emotions – releasing them with tears is a healthy reaction to loss.

We have chosen the experiences we'll go through in this lifetime. Not only will knowing this help you to understand and accept what happens in your life, but it can make a huge difference when it comes to dealing with the bad stuff that crops up.

Take time to just be with your family. Have everyone turn off their electronic devices and enjoy some no-screen time together – even if it's just for an hour or two.

We all need boundaries to ensure we don't get into a big mess running after the things that we think will make us feel better – the things that we think will kill our fear of life and death – but which don't really help us at all. Feeling better is when you sit and do your prayers or affirmations; when you connect with spirit and remind yourself that we are all surrounded by the white light of the Creator's unconditional love; when you tell your partner that you love them; when you seize life with courage. That is feeling better. You will find that your life no longer has any space for fear.

Tell your loved ones every day how much they mean to you. Part of being happy is to validate those around us, just as they validate us.

We are all connected to the spirit world. We all have what I describe as a big old tug-of-war rope that is coiled in our body and connects our physical body to our soul – like an umbilical cord. It's not a physical cord, but an energy mass. When we are young and strong, the rope is strong. When we are ill, the rope weakens until it is very flimsy. When the time is right, that connection will sever altogether, and that's when we cross over. Just like cutting an umbilical cord, it breaks away. You know how when a monarch butterfly is ready, it hatches and just breaks away from its chrysalis? It's the same scenario. I have seen it.

I know as well as anyone that life is hard sometimes. Challenging experiences help us to appreciate the good times, as well as the people in our life who support us through it all. There's a silver lining and a learning to be had from every experience, even though it may not feel like it at the time.

How much happier would our lives be if we had a little bit of guts? The guts to believe in ourselves, to lose our fear, to stop seeing ourselves as victims.

Not so many years ago I had nothing. I've been homeless. I grew up going barefoot to school. But now I'm living the dream. I'm doing what I love. I am complete. You, too, can live the dream. Once you're going in the right direction, everything will work out.

Forgiveness – great to learn, hard to master!

It's important that we don't get so mired in negativity that we can't even think of all the good things in life. When we get to rock bottom, spirit will send us some help.

Be assured that, when you pass, your soul has a chance to rejuvenate and be restored to full strength. So, when a person comes through in spirit, even if they were 89 when they took their last breath, and even if they had suffered from a debilitating illness, they will present themselves as full of beans. We all know that no one ever wants to get old. So when they come back and show me that they are full of energy, or beautiful and strong, with their health restored, we know that there is no suffering in spirit.

~

We're used to thinking that forgiveness is something we 'do' to someone else, or for someone else. On the surface this is true, but dig a little deeper and you'll see that forgiveness is really something we do for ourselves – a wonderful gift we can give ourselves.

True friends are one of life's greatest blessings. Appreciate those who are always there for you even when times are tough, and be sure to do the same in return.

We usually know when we've done wrong, don't we? If we are honest about how we feel, and about our relationships, I think we know whether there is anything we need to be forgiven for. It is a matter for our soul: I think of our soul as being our intuitive sense of right and wrong.

Spirit does not want us to be a victim, trapped by the behaviour of others, or trapped by our own negative thoughts and emotions. We are all in control of our own lives, far more than most of us realise. Because we are in charge of our own ideas and feelings, we are in charge of who we are – the kind of person we are.

I believe that when we experience *déjà vu*, it is where we have indeed already seen that situation before, when we chose our life's pathway. Your soul knows. *Déjà vu* is like your soul saying yes, you're on the right path, you're meant to be here. Whether it's a good story or not a good story, you're meant to be there to have the experience, to learn from it and move forward.

We all get stressed and drawn into business problems and life problems; we get busy and we forget about how beautiful this world can be. That's when meditation can bring us back and help us to appreciate the beauty that is all around us, and give us a sense of the full potential of our lives.

The incredible thing is that, even if we don't realise it, when we think of those who have passed, they are there.

Who are you? Why are you here? Are these not the big questions of our earthly life? When we come close to spirit, we approach answers to these questions.

Grief is a process, so don't beat yourself up for struggling to get over the loss of a loved one. Allow yourself to work through your grief, and then let that grief go. This does not mean forgetting that person – you can still honour their memory – but you must also move on with your life.

We all get stuck sometimes, and we get out of it by putting into action what we are thinking, instead of thinking in circles. Get off the sofa; make it happen. Get out there, put yourself out there, go for it.

There is always enormous relief in speaking the truth.

⁓

Feel like you are stuck in a rut? Sometimes moving on and making changes involves a big leap of faith, and I get that that can be scary. But don't go into it blind – do your homework and prepare for this new direction as best you can by doing training courses and asking for professional advice if necessary. The other thing you can do is ask spirit for guidance, then see what happens.

⁓

All the judgment we experience on this earthly plane falls away in the afterlife.

If you live in the past and the future, but scarcely stop to experience the present, let me tell you something really important: it is *now* that you will meet spirit. It's not in the past or in the future, but when you actually quieten down, sit in prayer or meditation, and anchor yourself in the most positive way to the present.

What if you could not only stop thinking negative thoughts, but actually start to fill your life with joy? If you can imagine it, you can make it happen. This is called 'visualisation', and it is extraordinarily powerful. It relies on your self-knowledge of how you want your life to be, in order for you to activate all your positive emotions.

Sometimes we are held back from spiritual development because we have unresolved feelings about our earthly relationships. When people pass, they have the opportunity to review their life on Earth, and sometimes they want to let their living loved ones know that they are now sorry for the way they conducted their earthly relationships. This can be hugely meaningful to the living, and can give them the ability to move on in life with renewed confidence, knowing they are loved. Far better, though, to live your life in a way that leaves no regrets.

If you choose to make your thoughts, feelings and actions work positively through your clarity, optimism and inspiration, you will raise your personal frequency towards that of the spirit realm. You will literally come closer to spirit.

Your thoughts are incredibly powerful –
they can even change your reality. If you
are always thinking negative thoughts, your
reality will be severely limited. Engage in
positive thinking, though, and you might be
surprised at the results.

Your hold inside you all sorts of dreams for a
life that's different to the one you have now.
But we often ignore our dreams. We tell
ourselves not to be silly, that we might fail,
that we don't deserve such achievements. As
humans we have been blessed with incredible
brains. Yet the left side of our brain can cause
us problems if we let it dictate the terms of
our life. How about listening to the right side
of your brain? Dare to dream and then let
your left side help you figure out the steps
you need to take to achieve your goal.

Often when we face serious setbacks, we become bitter and angry. We may feel that life is unfair, that God is unjust or does not exist. Our negativity ties us to the traumatic event, and we drag all that pain along with us into the future. It's important to realise that these reactions are choices that we make. Understandable, maybe, but still a choice, and not one that will help us in the long run. When life throws us challenges, we decide how we will respond. Hardships are always a spiritual challenge: will you shrink or grow? Will you turn away from spirit or move closer?

The power of our thoughts is an area in which we can be truly powerful in our own lives, if only we give ourselves permission to be. We can choose how we will be.

If anyone makes us feel as if our soul has been destroyed, they have gained control over us. How did they do this? The only possible answer is that we let them. And if we let them into our lives, we can also decide they no longer have any place with us. How do we do this without becoming bitter and carrying resentment around? The answer is, I believe, one of the great spiritual mysteries: forgiveness. It is the path to peace.

If we can forgive someone, we free our hearts. With forgiveness, resentment, anger and pain melt away. It is truly the most powerful form of love there is.

While the experiences that trigger your grief can be very different, the end result is usually pretty much the same. You become depressed and disillusioned, and you find it hard to get on with life. You cling to your memories of what you have lost – or your dreams of what should have been – and spend all your time thinking, 'If only . . .' You don't give 100 per cent of yourself to the things that matter, and you start missing out on experiences and relationships that could bring you happiness. In some cases, grief can become so overwhelming that it takes over everything and you are not living anymore, you are just existing. Understanding that the trauma you have been through is part of your journey, and then being able to let go of all the anguish, can make an incredible difference.

Becoming one with the universe and with spirit sounds so ultra-spiritual, but really it's just about acceptance – accepting the surroundings you are in, the car noises, the dog barking – so that these things don't interfere with your thoughts. We become aware of everything around us, we tune in to our surrounding frequencies, and in doing that our own frequency becomes really high and sensitive to spirit.

There are so many fears that hold us in place: fear of failure, of success, of being alone or abandoned, of rejection, of expressing our true feelings, of intimacy. And of course, the big one – fear of death. Don't let fear hold you back from living.

Sometimes people don't learn from their experiences, and so they go on repeating their mistakes and getting into more and more trouble. I believe we need experiences, good and bad, in order for us to learn. Life will throw us a curveball, and sometimes we don't rise to the challenge as well as we would hope. It becomes a problem, however, if you continue to repeat your bad experiences. Why aren't you learning? You let others down, and you let yourself down.

If you don't respect yourself, how can you expect anyone else to? Believe in yourself and know your own worth – you are precious, and anyone who doesn't understand that is not worth your time.

Much as we often want to, we can't take on the responsibility for other people's life path.

⌒

Feel like you've had a crummy day? Think about your week, and pick out all the positive things that have happened. If that's too hard, think about the last month, or the last year . . . You get the picture! Sometimes a bit of perspective will make a world of difference.

When we listen to spirit, when we connect to spirit with love, our lives become harmonious and meaningful, and we keep our feet and our hearts on the right path. Pay attention, listen to the messages of your body, and listen to the messages of your heart.

Overcoming fear and even rage, and adopting instead an attitude of acceptance and faith, can completely transform our experiences. An important point here is that acceptance is not passive. It is very, very active. It is not rolling over and giving up; it is grasping your challenges, looking them in the eye, acknowledging them, and dealing with them in an active, positive way.

It's okay to talk to your family in Heaven, to remember them, to acknowledge them and, obviously, to love them. But don't take this too far and behave almost as if the other person is still living. This drains the life out of both you and the people around you.

To be on your deathbed full of regret and doubt would be the worst thing – to wish you had done something else, but now it is too late. Isn't it worth facing your fears, replacing them with love and faith, in order to avoid that terrible scenario?

There's no room for resentment and spirit to co-exist. When you're feeling resentful and clingy, spirit gets pushed aside. When we find acceptance, we open up once again to all the possibilities of spirit. We feel spirit move once again in our hearts and, ironically, we are more connected to our loved ones than when we were clinging to them so relentlessly.

Spirit only want the best for us. They want us to be happy and to enjoy our lives. It is only when we accept their passing that they can truly find peace. So acceptance is a gift both for us and for our loved ones in spirit.

When we pay attention, we realise that all the little symbols and signs are spirit's way of communicating – the goosebumps, that feeling that someone is standing behind you even though there seems to be no one there, maybe a little shimmer or a shadow that you just catch out of the corner of your eye. It is spirit's way of attracting our attention, so that they can remind us that they are there, they love us, and they are not far away.

When we connect with spirit, we know in the deepest way we possibly can that all things are connected, and that we are connected to all things.

Love really is the bond that does not die. It never ceases to amaze me, the importance of these connections between people – the love we have for our parents even when we're getting old ourselves; the love we have for our children which never lessens in intensity, even after we've passed on; the way we keep alive the memory of our partner, even when they've gone years before. Humans really do have the most extraordinary capacity for love.

There's a very fine line between what we call reality and the spirit realm. Spirit can't be here 24 hours a day; they have lived their life in this physical existence. They're now in the afterlife, but their wairua, their spirit, is there for us. When we least expect it, they will be there for us.

Nobody's perfect. Remember this if a
loved one makes a mistake, and practise
forgiveness.

⁓

If you're going through a hard time, don't
keep it to yourself. Get it off your chest by
confiding in a friend.

⁓

Some people cling to the ones they love, even
when not letting go means they are pulling
everything down around them. They need
to learn what life is. It's just Nature being
Nature, and we need to accept that people do
pass on.

Cheering up a friend can work wonders in cheering yourself up, too.

Don't let other people's negativity get you down.

Make time to nurture your relationship. This could involve organising a romantic dinner out, or bringing your significant other breakfast in bed, or just making a point of telling your partner every day how much you love them.

There is one simple goal above everything else in spiritual awareness, and for us humans it's the hardest one of all: to love unconditionally. We love our children, our families, our friends – but what about the rest of the planet? To love unconditionally means to love without conditions: that is, no judgment, no ifs, buts or maybes. Much evil is done in the world through the negative judgments of one person or group over another. We can ask God, or spirit, to help free us from that negativity and to cultivate an attitude of acceptance and forgiveness – in a word, love.

When spirit pass on messages of love, reassurance and acknowledgement, they release the stresses, the pressure and the guilt. All those negative thoughts and doubts – the 'I should have, I could have, I would have' – just vanish. Spirit only want what's best for you.

If you have lost someone close to you and you are lonely, just remember that this feeling won't last forever. Don't push away your family and friends – remember how much they care for you, and that they only want what's best for you.

Non-judgment, forgiveness and love: these are the ultimate goals – and the ultimate challenges.

Losing a child has to be the worst experience anyone can go through. We all want to go before our kids – it just doesn't seem fair that their lives would be cut short. But it happens, and when it does I believe it is because of the journey that soul is on. I know I would be devastated, because my kids are the most important thing in my life. But I believe the Creator gives you a blessing in the child you are the mum or dad of, and if you lose them, it's because the Creator knows that you are strong enough to deal with it. And that little soul – whether they are six months old, six years old or 16 – if they go before you, they may just have earned their wings. They didn't need to stay long.

The path to spiritual connection is also a journey towards a better understanding of yourself. It can be no other way, for without that understanding of self, spirit can pull the wool over your eyes and lead you into places you might not want to go.

We can all connect with spirit. I'm not saying it's easy – it takes dedication, discipline and devotion, and it means stepping outside our daily business and distraction and actually making a time and a space for that spirit connection. But it's worth it.

Love continues even after the body's death, and love is the connection between this world and the next.

~

Practise gratitude in your everyday life. When something goes well for you – a social get-together, a business meeting, a harmonious exchange with your teenager – just say a quick 'thank you'. It is right to be thankful, and it also reminds us of the good in our life.

~

We must cherish every moment of time we have with the ones we love so that we can live without regret. It doesn't mean we won't miss them when they depart this life, but it helps to know that the love we had here on Earth continues in spirit.

I believe that before we were born into our physical bodies, we sat with the Creator and mapped out our life here on Earth. We chose the challenges, the things from which we need to learn – but as soon as we were born, we forgot. Our lives, with all their busy-ness and their material concerns, take us away from spirit. We forget that we are here to learn so that eventually we can achieve our angel wings and cease the cycle of reincarnation.

Making time in your daily life for spirit is part of awakening yourself to the wonders of life, the truth about the universe and your own place in it, and to your own potential.

Many of us live blindly, as if we think life goes on forever, and as if our chances to do the things we want, to have the relationships we want, are endless and limitless. Well, they are limitless, but they are not endless. If we can accept that we will pass, and that we don't know when we have chosen for that passing, it will help us live more fully.

We all need the support of friends and family. In your toughest times, your friends will lift you up, listen to you and embrace you.

Many of you reading this right now will recall put-downs or feelings of worthlessness you experienced when other people judged you for being different. Let those people inspire you to rise above their low opinions and to turn your life around, taking it in a positive direction. Thank them and forgive them.

Don't be one of those people who, on their deathbed, are filled with regret for the chances they never took. Instead of closing your mind, remain open to the limitless possibilities of the universe.

We all need good friends, so be grateful for the ones who have ended up walking with you through this life.

Spirit, the angels and the heavenly Father are always with us, and what a wonderful thing that is.

We never need to feel unloved, or even alone. When we remember those who have passed on, they are there for us, watching over us, and they want only the best for us.

Time and time again I do readings where I get spirit saying things to me along the lines of, 'Tell my daughter to stop doubting herself and do what she really wants to do. She's stuck in a rut; she needs to follow her passion.' Don't let fear of the unknown hold you back.

Whatever you are going through, it's okay to talk about it. Talking helps with the healing process – get it out in the open to start healing.

Always follow your dreams. Even if it scares you a little, or others don't approve, don't let this put you off – listen to your heart first and foremost, and allow yourself to live without regrets dragging you down.

The bond between you and your loved ones in spirit will bring you together again. You don't have to see them, you just have to think of them and they are there. Just because it's not physical and you can't actually see them standing in front of you doesn't mean they are not there. They are, and you can feel them in your heart.

Spirit is all around us. We just have to think of them, and those we have lost are with us. They are there when we are driving in the car and their favourite song comes on the radio. When we flick through photos and recall the good times we shared, they are by our side. When we cry because we miss them so much, they are next to us, wishing we could feel that they have their arms around us.

Life on the other side is uncomplicated and peaceful. It is beautiful.

We all make mistakes. It's what you do about them that counts. If you don't apologise for wronging someone, you will take that with you into the afterlife, and who wants that? Say sorry before you miss the chance.

~

It may seem a bit morbid, but it's important to consider what will happen when you pass on. Make sure you have a plan so that your family won't have the added stress of a financial burden at what will already be a difficult time. Perhaps even write letters to those closest to you, as a reminder of how you will always love them – even after you have left this Earth.

Losing a friend or family member is one of the most difficult things we will ever have to go through. In our grief, it can be easy to mourn the loss without remembering all the amazing experiences that person had – the times you were both bent over laughing together, the adventures you shared, and the many lives that person touched. It is so important to celebrate a life well lived.

You can still love someone who has passed and carry on with your life. Acceptance is one of the most important lessons we must learn in our time on this Earth. Life's far too short to dwell on what we cannot change.

So what's it like on the other side? What happens to us when we die? I can only assume from the glimpses I have been given thanks to spirit, but what I do know is that the realm of white light is an amazing place, and you will just have to take my word on that until you get there yourself.

Rushing around all day, every day, has become an accepted – even expected – way of life. In the afterlife, you can look forward to time being irrelevant. We should take this as a lesson to take things slower on this side, rather than forever trying to catch up on all that 'needs' to be done.

In the afterlife there are no physical elements. Your physical body exhausts itself and is left behind when you pass over. Your spirit, your white light – however you want to put it – is a speck of light, just a little wee speck, but inside is your whole soul and your soul's path; your previous journey and where it's probably going to go from here. All your memories – everything about your life from the places you went, the family you had, the work you did – are retained in the cellular memory inside this speck, ready for next time.

Throughout life, no matter our age, we are always learning.

In the old days we only had the daylight hours to do what we needed to – once it was dark, we got to rest. But these days with electricity we can keep going even in the hours of darkness. So we get out of our proper sleeping and working patterns, and we work longer hours. Is it any wonder people end up so stressed and anxious? Try fitting your schedule around daylight hours for a week, and see what a difference it makes.

When you cross over you will experience the Heaven you have set up for yourself. What you create there is determined by what you do here. If you throw garbage at life, then you will get garbage back. If you throw roses, then that's what will come back to you.

Have you ever met someone and within a really short time – or even instantly – it felt like you must have met before because you just seem to know each other really well? You get each other, something just clicks. I think this happens because you have had a past together somewhere. It's the soulmate thing.

You can talk to your loved one in spirit anytime you want. If you don't feel comfortable having a conversation with someone you can't physically see, try writing them a letter.

Ask yourself what you really want to do in this life. What job would make you the happiest person in the world? Yes, you have to pay the mortgage and the bills, but find something that will make you feel good. People worry about losing money, but I believe that if you do what you love, the money will follow.

Part of taking charge of your life can mean learning to let go. This is a very important lesson, and something that a lot of people struggle with. Letting go can mean lots of things. It can mean letting go of issues in your life that you haven't got over, and are holding onto. All they do is drag you down, and you need to get rid of them.

Money, power, fame – so many people wish for these, without realising that they alone will never make you feel fulfilled. Learning lessons, having healthy relationships and self-realisation are what life is really all about.

Life is about good times as well as bad, laughter as well as tears.

Keep your heart open, forgive where you can and remember to stay calm – for it was all planned out before you came here. Let it be.

Whether you wish to surrender negativity, forgive those who have hurt you, accept what is happening in your life or learn to love yourself, you can do all of this with meditation. Start meditating daily, and you will soon experience results.

⁓

I know the pain people go through when they have lost someone special to them, because I feel their pain. So often people want to numb it, and they turn to alcohol and drugs. Please trust me when I say that these will never take away the pain – they will only make things worse. Have faith that this is all part of God's plan.

Every once in a while, take a moment to just be. Find a quiet place to relax – whether it's in the garden, alongside a river or simply on the couch at home. Put aside all your worries and clear your mind. This is the basis of meditation, and of finding peace within yourself.

You may feel like you have lost your way, but have faith that this is temporary. Spirit will lead you back to your life's path when the time is right.

If you can't get your head around the idea of starting up a conversation with someone you can't see as they have crossed over, give this a go: write down what each of you might say if you were sitting there face to face, having a friendly chat over a cup of tea. Keep writing down what you would be likely to say to each other if you could, and there you are, you are having a conversation. You might be surprised at where it takes you, and how much comfort you get.

Know that everything that happens will be for a reason. Learn whatever lessons are in store for you and be forgiving to all.

Accept that everything is part of your journey – you chose to marry that person, or be their parent or child. Yes, it still breaks you to pieces that you have lost them, or their life was cut short. But understanding the journey can give meaning to a death that can otherwise seem totally random, unfair, sad and sometimes even downright cruel.

Don't give up hope when it feels like everything is just too hard. Do whatever you need to do to feel better: talk to your loved ones in spirit, meet with a friend, pray, meditate – we all need to learn how to cope through difficult times.

I know it is something I tend to say over and over, but we really can all feel the presence of those in the afterlife. If it was a child, maybe read them some of the bedtime stories they always used to love. If you and your mum used to make a point of sitting down together to watch *Coronation Street*, whenever that distinctive theme tune starts playing, spend a few moments thinking about Mum and how she used to laugh at that lady with the curlers in her hair and the ducks on her wall. When you do that, she will be with you.

Getting back to Nature soothes the soul. My happy place is out on the ocean fishing, but yours might be sitting alongside a river or camping under the stars. Whatever it is you enjoy doing in Nature, be sure to make time for it.

We are here to learn lessons – things like learning to stand up for ourselves, or conquering anger, or being able to forgive. When we have absorbed each of these lessons, we can then tick them off the list and move on to the next thing. We can't usually learn everything we need to in one lifetime, so we keep coming back to try to achieve the goals we have set for ourselves. If we don't manage to learn a particular lesson in this life, we will get it again in the next life, and again and again, until we finally nail it. There's no getting out of these lessons – they are written.

When someone close to us dies, their soul lives on in the afterlife, which is a beautiful place full of love.

Each time we come back to this side of life, we are slightly more evolved. Ever known one of those children who seem unusually advanced for their age? They seem to cruise through life without too many hassles, and they are so much more mature than other kids their age. These are typical traits of an old soul. They're well on their way to becoming an angel, and this could even be their last time here before getting their wings. Then there are those who are the complete opposite – the young souls. They're always in trouble and they seem to learn the hard way. It might take them a few more return journeys before they get their wings. Whether you're an old soul or a young one, we all have lessons to learn – but the incredible thing is that we are on the path to becoming an angel.

As long as it is part of your journey, your family in spirit can help you out where necessary – they have the ability to do that. When you're feeling lost, look out for signs from spirit.

Where is Heaven? Where do we actually go when we die? And what is it really like? The answer is Heaven is all around us. The thing is, it's just on a different frequency to the one where we are. And what is it like, being there? In a word, beautiful. Absolutely, utterly, incredibly, beyond-words beautiful.

The unconditional love of spirit is within easy reach of us all, if we just know how to access it. Open yourself to spirit.

Sadly, there are quite a lot of people out there who have very low self-worth and have turned their backs on love. Our Creator wants us all to be able to go home, to the white light, or to Heaven, if you like. But to do that, you need to be able to love. Work on unconditionally loving yourself and others.

Sometimes when really awful things happen to good people it is an indication that they are very close to becoming an angel. Quite often, those people who seem really nice and cool and kind are evolved souls who are not all that far off getting their angel wings, but first they have to go through a pretty steep learning curve. They'll go through these terrible experiences so it can help them to relate to others once they have their wings.

There is a lesson to be had in every experience, and in some cases it is not just those who are directly involved who learn, but those who hear about it.

The loss of a pet can be devastating. Pets add to our lives in so many ways – they are our companions and confidants, they make us laugh and they ease any suffering we experience. Remember the good times and hold onto those memories – don't let thoughts of illness towards the end, or of having to put them down, be all you think about.

In case you haven't realised by now, life is not always fair. Sometimes it sucks big time. Bad things do happen to good people – and vice versa. Between what has been set down for us to experience and karma, there are reasons why things happen that might not seem fair. And getting upset and angry is an obvious response when things don't work out the way we want them to, or something terrible takes place. But there's no point in letting it take over your life. Constantly asking 'Why? Why? Why?' will not get you anywhere. It will just do your head in. It happened, you can't change it. But you can change how you respond to it, and how you move forward.

Spirit will do what they can to ease our path. I always ask spirit for protection for my family, especially while I'm away on the road touring. I say a little prayer before I go, asking that they be kept safe. When I'm driving long distances or going out fishing or diving, I imagine the car or boat bathed in protective white light, and I know that spirit is looking after me. You, too, can ask spirit to watch over you and your loved ones.

Be patient. In this fast-paced world we want everything to happen right away, but if you just let go and accept that things will happen when they're supposed to, life will go so much more smoothly.

When your time comes, crossing over is the most amazing feeling. You feel incredibly calm and at peace. Any pain and fear you have disappears, and you are wrapped in pure love. I've had a few near-death experiences in my lifetime, and each time has reinforced my belief that when we die we go home, and it is an incredible feeling.

⁓

There's no doubt about it: loss hurts. Everyone deals with loss in their own way, but I believe understanding that everything happens because it was meant to is the first step to accepting the death of someone you love.

It's easy to follow the crowd and just do what everyone else is doing, but is it right? Is it who you are? Is it what you know to be true? Don't go along with something just for the sake of it, because eventually it will come back to bite you on the backside. You may think you are doing what's best for a peaceful life or to make somebody else happy, but what you are doing is lying to yourself. And good luck living with yourself if you do that.

You may feel angry after losing someone – especially if they died unexpectedly – but it's important not to let this feeling linger as it doesn't achieve anything. Your loved one in spirit would not want you to be feeling that way.

For many of us, losing someone is the biggest, saddest, most tragic thing that happens in our lifetime. The sense of loss can be overwhelming and can affect everything we do. Grief is a natural part of loss and we all need to go through it, but hanging on to it and letting it take over your life is not what we're meant to be doing. Allow yourself to move on.

Spirit don't want us to stop living our lives because we're mourning them. I have spirit telling me time and time again that, while they are happy that their loved ones in this world still remember and love them, they aren't pleased when missing them consumes you. They want you to remember them with a smile as you get on with life.

I've been rejected and I know how much it hurts. The despair of not being wanted can stay with you for years, if you let it. It's hard not to take rejection personally. You do think that it is something to do with you, that you're not good enough, or you've screwed up in some way. Have some self-belief! Just because one person has decided you are not the one for them, it does not mean you are not worthy. Get back out there and find someone better! You deserve to be happy.

Sometimes we need to understand that taking a new path means starting at the beginning. You may struggle initially, but overcoming challenges is what leads to success.

Naturally, in our society we need money to survive. We need to feed the kids; we need houses, cars, all these things in life. And to get those things we have to work. But how many people are happy at their job? The only people I have ever met who are truly happy are the people who do what they love, whose 'work' reflects something fundamental about them. This is what we should all aim for.

Every day, you should be stretching yourself to become the best version of yourself that you can be.

When I tell people that the whole point of us being here is to learn lessons, you can see some of them stifling a groan. They thought they'd escaped lessons when they left school! Well, I'm sorry, people, but that's the way it is. You were the one who sat down with our Creator at the beginning of your existence to decide what you needed to learn, and you will keep getting those lessons until you can tick them all off and say 'Done!' And at the end, you'll get angel wings and become one of those incredibly evolved souls who stay in this wondrous place we call Heaven instead of having to tough it out here. You'll also get to pop back here whenever you want, to use your abilities to help out people on this side of life.

If you ignore your problems, they will only get worse – and so will your stress levels! I know it can be tough, but face up to your issues and you will be feeling carefree and relaxed before you know it.

Material possessions are not what life is all about. If you are working so hard to pay off the mortgage and the car that you never see your family, and when you go on holiday you are so exhausted you spend all your time sleeping, then there is something wrong somewhere. And if you are not happy about what you are doing, but you keep going because you need to upgrade to the newest model of your car, then it is time for a reality check. It's just stuff; is it really that important?

Making mistakes is part of being a human. However, you shouldn't be making the same mistakes over and over again. If you keep having to pay a huge amount in bank fees because you are continually overdrawn, you are not learning. If you are constantly passed over for promotion in favour of one of your workmates because you are too shy to claim credit for the great ideas you come up with, you are not learning . . . See where I am going with this? It may be time for you to learn a few more lessons.

Life is an amazing blessing. Be sure to cherish it every day.

Being true to yourself is not always the easy option. For example, if you have refused to acknowledge that you are gay and you got married and had kids, you may not want to admit the truth because you know it is going to cause your partner and kids a lot of pain. You can't bear to put them through that. But in the meantime your whole relationship is based on a lie. And that's not right. Being true to yourself may be the right option, but, to be honest, it is not always the easy one.

Enjoy your life! I meet so many people who work until they drop, instead of spending precious time with their family and friends. Life's too short to spend every moment working.

Kindness and compassion are two of the most important virtues you can have.

For me, compassion means opening your heart to someone else, and feeling for them. Kindness usually follows on from compassion – it means doing things for people because you care and want to help make things better for them. It doesn't hurt to spend a few moments of your time doing something for others. It can be something as simple as ringing your auntie to see how she is doing, or volunteering to cut your neighbour's hedge because you know they struggle with it now that they're getting on a bit.

There are people out there who are champions at burying their heads in the sand. They think if you just push a problem to one side, it will go away. Sorry, but it won't! Face up to your problems.

If you didn't have to worry about earning a living, what would you do with your life? Well, if that's what you really want to do, if that's what would make you happy, why don't you do it? There are always plenty of excuses – but in many cases, where there's a will, there's a way.

Stand up for yourself. This can range from something fairly minor, like speaking out when someone criticises your opinion, through to the more major stuff, like refusing to stay with a partner who knocks you about. Know when to say that enough is enough.

One of the first things that is drummed into us as kids is that it is important to tell the truth. But often, as we get older, we start seeing bending the truth as a useful way of covering our tracks. We don't want to get in trouble, we don't want to upset someone or we don't want to face up to something, so we lie. But one thing I have learned from the work I do is that the truth will prevail in the end. We can't hide the truth from our Creator, or from spirit. They know. And at the end of the day, you know, too, and you have to live with the consequences of not telling the truth.

Some people are sceptical when I tell them that whenever we think of those we have lost, they will be with us. 'Isn't it just my imagination, though?' I am asked. No, it isn't. As soon as you bring them to mind, they will be by your side.

If you are going through a really tough time, particularly when it comes to losing someone, find the strength to deal with it by understanding that it's part of your – and your loved one's – journey. Don't get me wrong; you can still be desperately sad and wish things could have been different. You can still hurt. But keep going, even if it is just taking it one day or even one hour at a time.

After having lost someone, you may find yourself wondering how a whole personality could be snuffed out, just like that. Their body may no longer work, but what has happened to their soul, the essence of them? Where are they? They are in the afterlife, in the white light. They have gone through the light and some of them may have even gone up the stairs to get their wings. They have also been to the healing rooms, and are free of the pain and trauma. Their injuries are gone and they are fine. I have been shown this time and time again by spirit.

We all go through tough times. When that happens, it can be easy to wallow in being a victim. But don't let the hardships you have suffered define you! You are so much more than that.

Everyone has good days and bad days. There are times when you'd probably give anything for an easy life. But when you look back at occasions that have seemed impossibly hard, and reflect on how you came through them stronger, wiser and with greater faith, I hope you will know that you just have to keep going.

What do you have to do today? Just put one foot in front of the other. It's okay to grieve, but don't let it stop you from having a happy, fulfilling life – trust in the Creator and keep going.

You never know what's around the corner, so take nothing for granted. Be grateful for all that you have been blessed with in this life.

I hope I can adequately convey the message from spirit that there is nothing to fear in death. If there is anything we should be afraid of, it is not living life to the fullest. It is of not spending time with the people we love, and of not doing our best to learn the lessons we are given.

Most of all, our existence is about love. It's about having love for each other, for this amazing world, for our Creator and for ourselves.

What spirit really want is for you to live your life to the fullest.

To all the souls who we have loved and lost to the light in our lifetime, we miss you all very much. However, we trust you are with us, surrounding us with your love every day.

It may comfort you to realise that when someone dies, it doesn't have to be goodbye. Just think of that person, and they will be with you. Just because they are no longer on this Earth doesn't mean that the bond you shared is gone. They still want you to be happy and lead a fulfilling life.

Spirit are all around us. Our loved ones are still there, just not in the same way they were before they passed. That can give us so much comfort and help to ease the pain when we suffer a loss.

We can't see the wind, yet we know it exists. We can feel it; we can see the effects it has. It is the same with spirit. You may not be able to see them, or sense them particularly well, but trust me, they're there. We are surrounded by spirit.

Ever wonder why you're here on this Earth? It's simple: you are here to grow and develop, to love and be loved, to enjoy all that this life has to offer. Make the most of every moment.

Here's what I believe: at the beginning of our existence, we sit down with the Creator to map out our journey through life, the ultimate goal being to learn lots of lessons and eventually become angels so we can stay in the amazing place full of love called Heaven. We're then born as physical beings, and off we go through life. Along the way we should be learning the lessons we set ourselves, and if we don't tick them all off in this lifetime, we come back for another go at it. When each lifetime on this Earth comes to an end, our souls become specks of light that cross into the white light on the other side. We hang out in Heaven until we are ready to come back here and continue on our journey towards earning our angel wings.

Spirit don't always send us the signs we might be expecting or hoping for, but they do have remarkable ways of letting us know they are there.

~

Spend a lot of time laughing and playing, even as an adult. This will help to keep you sane even through the worst of times.

~

If only we as a human race could love each other more. Wouldn't the world be a much better place?

When we die we don't cease to exist, we just go somewhere else. And we can pop back to this side of life to see our family and friends and be around them. We can even help them out with everyday life if they realise that we are there, and they ask for help. Isn't that good to know?

Our Creator wants us all to end up in the light. Our Creator is all-loving and is prepared to forgive us if we ask for it. Forgiveness is all part of the experience. If we ask for forgiveness and are prepared to change, we will be accepted into the white light. The door is always open; it is just up to us whether we are prepared to walk through it or not.

Make an effort to see your friends even when you are feeling down. You may not want to leave the house, but it's amazing how much better you will feel after a catch-up with a loved one.

One of the things I often get from spirit is that they wish they had done certain things before they crossed over, like make sure their family knew how much they loved them. That's why it is important to tell those you love how you feel, and show them, too. Don't put it off – you don't know what is around the corner.

You may not realise it, but people are often surrounded by spirit. If the loved ones you have lost are with you in your thoughts and your heart, you are never alone.

When I talk about dying and going into the afterlife, I usually refer to stepping into the light. For most of us, that's what happens. I have been shown where we go, and it is a beautiful place, bathed in white light. This is where we rest and recuperate from whatever it was that caused our death, and where we prepare to return to this side of life, if there are still things we need to achieve on our life's path. Once we have gotten our angel wings, we can stay in this place of bliss permanently.

Do you have a particularly close relationship with one of your siblings, or an old school friend? Did you instantly bond with a workmate from the first day on the job? Chances are you were family, great mates, or even married in a previous life. Your soul remembers that relationship and you feel a real closeness to that person for no apparent reason.

It can feel like a huge weight has been lifted when you come to accept that the person you love hasn't really left you. They're still there, albeit in a slightly different way to the way they used to be. And while you can't hug them, you can still talk to them, and you can still feel their love.

You have to stop putting so much pressure on yourself, and start believing in yourself.

⟋⟍⟋

We each have a book up in Heaven that contains all the details of our life. It sits on a kind of pulpit, surrounded by misty cloud. Our name and date of birth are inscribed on the cover, and every page relates to a day in our lives, and every chapter is a year. The lessons we are to experience are already written, so we must learn them or we will have no choice but to repeat them over and over again.

⟋⟍⟋

Make time for your kids. You don't want to be coming through in the afterlife saying 'I'm sorry I let my child down.' Do something about it now, because one day it will be too late.

When someone you love goes into the light, it can be devastating regardless of the circumstances. All I can say is that if they were still meant to be alive, they would be. You've heard me say this over and over, but here it comes again: this is part of their journey, and of yours, too. That tests a lot of people's faith, but it is something you have to accept, as hard as that might seem.

Keep a journal beside your bed, so you can write down your dreams first thing in the morning. Recording your dreams can help you to remember them more easily and also pick up messages from spirit – often they will communicate with us via our dreams.

Don't beat yourself up over the little things that aren't important in the grand scheme of things. Be kind to yourself, and remember that you are only human.

Too often we think we are bulletproof, or that if we don't face up to a problem – and I'm talking about emotional issues here as well as health ones – it will go away. It won't. It will most likely get worse. And then you'll be well and truly stuffed. We need to face up to things.

You only get to stay permanently in Heaven once you get your angel wings. When you have got them, you can stay in the white light for all eternity. You have achieved everything you set out to do, you have worked hard and now you get your reward. And believe me, from what I have seen of Heaven, once you get there you just won't want to go anywhere else.

Believe in yourself. You don't need to compete with others; you are naturally beautiful.

Depression and anxiety are not about a lack of strength or toughness; they are illnesses that make people unwell. In the worst-case scenario, mental health problems can lead to suicide. Because of what I do for a living, I come into contact with a lot of people whose lives have been devastated by suicide. I not only see how families are left heartbroken having lost someone this way, but I see how it has affected the person who killed themselves when they come through to me in spirit. It's so incredibly painful to lose someone that way, but the good news is that the experiences they have had all count towards them eventually getting their angel wings one day.

If you want to try to connect with a family member you have never met, it helps to have a photo of the person so you can visualise them. Just sit down somewhere quiet, close your eyes and think about what you know about that person. If you don't get any signs from them, or if the signs you do get don't mean anything, don't worry. It might take a while to develop a connection – just try again. But one thing I can assure you of – your relative will be happy that you are trying to get in touch. He or she will have been watching you from Heaven.

To get your angel wings, you have got to tick certain lessons off a list, and, until you have managed to do that, you have to keep coming back to learn them.

Do you repeatedly find yourself in situations where you let people walk all over you? You know you should learn to stand up for yourself, but that takes courage you just don't have. If you get to the end of this life and are still being a doormat, then – guess what? – you're going to keep coming back here and being constantly challenged until you learn how not to let people walk over you.

Pop a small notebook in your handbag to jot down thoughts or occurrences that might have a spiritual connection. Writing things down helps you to clarify your feelings, and perhaps see that coincidences aren't so coincidental after all.

Your body is just a vessel. When you cross over to the other side, you leave behind your physical body. It has served its purpose and doesn't work anymore, and you go back to being a speck of light. This is your soul; this is who you are – your body was just the casing that has been housing it.

~

Don't compare your life with anyone else's. We all have our own path to follow, and in our own journey everything will take place exactly when and how it is supposed to.

If you don't accept that someone close to you has crossed into the light, you'll get stuck. You'll go over and over the loss, desperately wishing things could be different, when, sadly, they can't be. Often you start blaming people. You need to move on from finding someone to blame. Remember, it is what it is.

If you feel like you are having the worst day, put things in perspective. Think about whether this will even be a blip on the radar a few years down the track – it might surprise you to realise what's truly important, and what can just be put down to a bad day that's almost over anyway.

Rarely is the path we are on through life straight and smooth. It tends to veer all over the place, and the sooner we can accept and embrace that, the better.

Spirit fills us with love and the knowledge of love, and that knowledge brings us a great feeling of purpose. When I communicate with spirit, I feel whole – my own soul feels full, happy and right. I tune into all the good things of life: peacefulness, joy, love. It is an expanded feeling. I begin to feel at one with the world. You can connect with spirit, too, by sitting in a quiet place and cherishing your memories of those who have passed.

Sometimes you just have to take that first
step by trying something new. Yes, you
might fail, but at least you tried. At least you
weren't afraid of change. Making changes
does often involve courage. It takes guts
to go and ask your boss for a pay raise.
You have to be brave to plough all of your
savings into your own business. But it might
just change your life for the better, so isn't it
worth taking the chance?

Spirit can work in ways that really are quite
amazing. Next time your intuition is proved
correct, or you experience a really weird
coincidence, just say a little thank you. You
had a helping hand.

Is there an issue you feel really strongly about? Maybe you are concerned about the terrible rates of child abuse, or housing, or climate change. If there is something that you think is important, don't just sit at home muttering about it. Go to rallies, sign petitions, write letters to politicians, post about it on social media. If only we all stood up in support of causes we believed in, we'd have a very powerful force for change.

Don't hold grudges against those who have wronged you. I know, I know – easy to say, difficult to do! Try to clear the air by talking through any issues you have, and if the other person isn't willing to work on your relationship, at the very least you'll be able to walk away with a clear conscience.

Some people not only embrace change, they actively go after it. But then there are others who are scared of change and want everything to stay exactly as it is. They like their home, their job, their lifestyle. There's nothing wrong with this – if all these things make them happy, then that's a good thing. But when something happens that is out of their control, and their nice cosy life gets turned upside down, they freak out. In a situation like this, you need to accept what is happening and make the best of it. This is part of your journey, so go with it. If you are having trouble dealing with these changes, ask spirit to show you the positives. You just never know what might happen.

Whenever you do something wrong, own up to your mistake and apologise if the situation calls for it. Take ownership of your own actions and the choices you have made.

Close friends and family members who have passed are there in your thoughts and your heart, and they are there alongside you even through the hardest of times. You are still connected to each other; it is just a little different to the way it was when they were here with you physically. When you think of that person you love you can feel that bond, the same as you could feel it when they were still here. And they can feel it, too.

The one thing that is consistent in life is change. Whether we like it or not, things do change, so you need to make the best of it.

I believe acceptance is the key to dealing not only with grief, but with everything that life throws at us. Understand that once something takes place, you can't change it. You can't turn the clock back. What you can do is choose to accept that this is your path. You can decide to acknowledge it for what it is, and keep moving forward.

Where there's life, there's death. At times it may feel like everything is sad, but remember that balance is a sure thing in this world. Happy times are probably right around the corner.

For many of us, our relationships with our pets is among the most important, if not the most important, things to us. It's easy to understand why: animals offer us unconditional, uncomplicated love. They're loyal and true, always comforting and, especially for people who live alone, they fill up your life. Treasure your time with pets.

Isn't it comforting to know that those you have lost are okay, and that one day you will see them again? Don't forget they miss us as much as we miss them. Yes, they're in the beautiful place that Heaven is, but their hearts ache for you, too. Tell them you love them, and you'll help to ease the pain they feel from being separated from you.

To me, love is what really matters, it's what we're here for. Love is what keeps us connected to our friends and family members even when they're dead – it creates a bond that cannot be broken.

Sometimes life throws challenges at us that shake our beliefs. Keeping your faith isn't always easy, but you will be so much stronger and better off for it.

Gratitude is key. Be grateful for your family, friends, health . . . the list goes on. Focus on the positives in your life.

Trust me, when you learn to accept that what has taken place is part of your journey through life, then dealing with the loss of a loved one, and so many other challenges, will become easier to bear.

Take charge and don't blame others for what is happening in your life. If you are in a relationship that is making you miserable and bad-tempered and horrible to your kids, do what you can to fix it. If you can't fix it, get out of it. By staying, what are you doing with your life? You are wasting years of precious living. What are you teaching your kids? What is it doing to them, seeing you fighting and being miserable? What's it like for them when there is no love in your home? Yes, it is very difficult to end a relationship when there are kids involved, but what you are doing by staying is teaching them to pretend to be happy and to lie. And you need to think about your own sanity, too.

After the loss of a loved one, remember that others are hurting, too. Be kind to one another. At times, focusing on the wellbeing of your family or friends can help you to work through your own grief as well.

～

Not everyone in our lives is meant to be there a long time. Be it a young child, a pet or a new friend, if you had only a short time with someone, cherish your memories. They are no less significant or treasured simply because you had them in your life only briefly. Time is irrelevant when it comes to love.

Make an effort to laugh and smile often. These actions are infectious, so they will cheer up those around you – and you might be surprised by how much happier they will make you, too.

If you think you are not good enough, then you aren't going to achieve all you could. You are holding yourself back. Love yourself, and always know that you are worthy.

Children have their own journeys to make. We can be here to guide them if they need it, but we can't tell them what to do. They have to make their own choices. We're here as parents to make sure they don't do anything harmful or dangerous, but they have to find their own path.

Don't stay in a job if it makes you unhappy. How many people spend Sunday night with a sick feeling in their gut, knowing that they have to go to work the next day? If you do choose to stay in a job you don't like, make the most of it. Change your attitude, and find something to like about it.

Looking back over history can be quite disheartening. When you read up or watch TV documentaries about wars, you're left thinking, 'Why do we do this to ourselves over and over again? How many more people have to lose their lives?' What we should be learning from war is that instead of trying to wipe each other off the face of the planet, we should be learning to 'love thy neighbour' and respect our differences so that we can live side by side.

Feeling guilty is a waste of time. If you can learn something from an experience, do so, but don't dwell on what you can't change.

You are only in this physical body once. It is your responsibility to do it well.

～

Embrace change. Trust that whatever happens is part of your journey.

～

There is no reason to be afraid of dying. Death may take you to another place, but it is a beautiful, wondrous environment where you will feel no pain. And when it is your time to go, you will even be able to watch over your friends and family from Heaven.

If something keeps happening to you, it may be a lesson you need to learn. Some of you might wonder, 'How come every guy I end up with is a scumbag who treats me like rubbish?' Stop and think about it for a minute. How often has this happened? Do you always go for the same types? If you can see a pattern, then ask yourself what it is about you that continually attracts losers, and whether there's something you can change. Start by deciding that you're not going to hang around if they treat you badly. Remind yourself that you don't deserve this. Value yourself. Take steps to change things, and you won't get that lesson again.

If only we could be more like our pets: loving one another unconditionally, exhibiting loyalty and trust – wouldn't the world be a much simpler place?

Selfless acts can be the best therapy. When you're grieving, or feeling rejected, or simply having a sad day, try cheering yourself up by doing something nice for a friend. It's amazing how a simple act of kindness can make someone's day – and you might just find that your own problems don't seem so bad anymore.

Laughter is an amazing healer. If you're feeling down, try relaxing in front of a sitcom or reading a humorous book – it's incredible how a bit of laughter can make you feel better.

Trust takes time to build up, but can be shattered so quickly. If someone has broken your trust in them, your relationship will struggle. Allow that person to attempt to earn your trust again, but if you find that doesn't work, it's time to walk away.

Use a journal to jot down your innermost thoughts each day – your hopes, goals, gratitudes, miseries. The healing power of putting your most private ideas down on paper is incredible.

I am blessed to walk in the white light – the unconditional love of the angels, of Jesus, God, the Creator, the Universe – whatever expression you prefer. The white light is your saviour. Honour it until you cross into it; until you return home to the angels forever.

Meditation doesn't have to involve chanting a mantra or years of practice. It can be as simple as finding a quiet place in the fresh air to sit, close your eyes and breathe. Just breathe, and empty your mind as best you can.

Believe it or not, happiness requires effort. If you truly want to be happy, work towards it by expressing gratitude every day, demonstrating kindness to others, and making an effort to smile and laugh as much as possible.

When you wake up each morning, take a moment to reflect on what you want to achieve in the day ahead. Visualisation is an amazing tool.

Whenever you meet someone new, rather than forming an immediate judgment, give them a chance to prove themselves.

Love yourself. You are incredible and one-of-a-kind, but sometimes you will need to remind yourself of that fact. Just think of all you have achieved, and all the lives you have enriched simply by being you.

Do you ever find yourself holding onto the past, to situations that were once a big part of your life? Things change and you can't live in the past forever. You may realise deep down that the time to move on has come, but you still cling to how things were. Instead, accept that that phase of your life is over and move forward.

If someone is causing you emotional pain, have the courage to confront them. It may be that they don't realise the effect they are having on you, and talking it through with them will clear the air and lift a weight from your shoulders. If you don't chat to them, you may become bitter and resentful – and who wants to feel that way?

Nourish your relationships, so your loved ones know how much you care. There's no better gift you can give than your time.

⁓

When you go to bed tonight, reflect on everything you have achieved today. Even the smallest of things – like making a colleague smile, or cooking something you know your kids love to eat – should be celebrated.

Learn to stand up for yourself. Decide that today will be the day you stop letting people walk all over you. Only you have the power to do this – you can't control how others treat you, but you can change what you do about it.

Don't hold onto destructive emotions like anger. Does getting angry help in any way? Does it make you feel better? No – in fact, often it will escalate a situation from bad to worse, and leave you feeling even more upset. Instead of allowing anger to take over, take a deep breath and count to 10 to calm yourself down.

Accept that you can't always get what you want. This isn't to say you shouldn't work hard to achieve your goals, but if something isn't written into your journey you must make the best of it and move on.

Some people are meant to be in our lives long-term; others will just pass through. It can be tricky recognising the difference, but if it is just a short-term thing, you need to accept it for what it is. Don't hang on for dear life – the one who will end up getting hurt the most is you. Step back and just let it go.

Complaining gets you nowhere. However, expressing your feelings clearly and constructively, and standing up for yourself, does.

It's only natural to feel insecure now and again, but if this feeling is overwhelming your life you must do something about it. Your thoughts are your reality, so make an effort to think positively.

Live each day as it comes. Worrying about what's ahead will only make you anxious, and doesn't actually achieve anything.

When we do wrong – behave dishonestly, especially in our family relationships and friendships – we usually know. In fact, no one will probably be harder on us than we are on ourselves. Right your wrongs and feel the weight melt from your shoulders.

⁓

If you fail at something, don't lose heart. Instead, view the experience as a lesson learnt, and a step on the path towards success.

Healing won't happen overnight. I know
it's hard – sometimes it's the hardest thing
in the world – but you must allow yourself
time to grieve after a loss. Don't expect to feel
like yourself again right away, but do expect
to reach a stage of acceptance and know
happiness again.

Face your problems head-on. Running away
will only prolong an issue – better to confront
the situation and be able to move on.

You shouldn't have to convince someone to like you – either they do or they don't, and if they don't that's their loss. There's no point in wasting time trying to please someone who doesn't appreciate you.

Instead of rushing into something, sit back a moment and ensure your decision will be a wise one.

Making goals can feel overwhelming unless you break them down into easily achievable aims.

I have lost track of the times spirit people have said to me during readings, 'Tell my mum and dad I'm fine, I'm happy, I miss them and I know they miss me, but they need to get on with life and be happy again.' And it's not unusual for dead people to want their partners to find someone new who will make them happy. That's not betraying your partner or saying your relationship with them doesn't mean anything. Of course it does, and you will always carry them in your heart. But you are still here in this world with the rest of your life to get on with, and nobody wants you to be miserable – least of all them. Harmony and happiness are what we are trying to achieve. And sometimes to do that, we have to let go.

Before you yell at your partner, or send off that angry email to a colleague, or snap at the supermarket checkout operator, stand back a moment and consider: does this situation really call for me losing my temper? Give it a moment and you might find it's not such a big deal after all. Getting angry doesn't solve anything; in fact, it will probably make the situation even worse.

Be kind to yourself. This can be as simple as allowing yourself time to kick back with a cuppa, or to laze in a bubble bath, or even just order takeaways so you get a night off from cooking and dishes.

Negativity will only make you feel worse about a situation. Be positive in all that you do – it might surprise you how great you'll feel as a result.

Remember to say 'thank you'. It amazes me how we try so hard to instil good manners in our children, but then forget to be polite ourselves!

Hugs are really important. Humans need touch, especially when you are going through a tough time and need a reminder that you have support.

It's impossible to please everyone. Stop wasting your time trying to keep all the people around you happy, and start concentrating on doing what's right for you.

Bad habits can be really hard to break, I know. Start by identifying what you need to work on, and then come up with a game plan for changing your habit over time. It might not happen right away, but with a bit of time you can create a healthy new normal.

Remember as a kid how you would sometimes laugh so hard you cried? Try to capture that carefree joy again as an adult.

⁓

There are so many ways to show your love other than showering someone with expensive gifts. Don't get me wrong, I love giving and receiving a good present now and again, but material possessions are not the be-all and end-all. Often a thoughtful gift that has cost you nothing but time is the most appreciated.

If you find yourself always arguing with your partner or a particular friend, take a moment to step back from the situation. Ask yourself: 'Could I act in a more positive way to reduce the tension between us?' When you're angry, it's easy to ignore your own actions and focus only on what the other person is doing wrong.

Live in the moment! I know, easier said than done, but it's so important not to dwell on the past – after all, you can't change it.

It is terrible when someone passes with words unspoken, and past wrongs unforgiven. People find it very hard to move on with their lives in these circumstances. And, of course, the hardest thing of all can be to forgive ourselves when we have wronged someone. The answer is to use your spiritual practice of prayer and meditation to get close to spirit, to feel the pure love of spirit, and to release your feelings of self-blame.

Don't let grief or fear drag you down. Always stay hopeful about what life has in store for you in the years to come. Life is meant to be lived!

Do you think it was just random that you happened to get chatting to some guy in the supermarket checkout and then he asked you out for a drink sometime? Or that you popped in to see some friends and their newly single next-door neighbour just happened to be there? Your paths crossed because they were meant to. You chose this person to be in your life way back when you mapped out your whole journey. People find it hard to grasp this concept if in the end the relationship is not all sunshine and roses, but you need to realise that person was a part of your life for a reason. Maybe that reason was to give you your beautiful kids. Maybe it was to teach you to stand up for yourself. They are – or were – in your life to help you learn the lessons you chose for yourself.

On this journey, the most important thing you can have is an open mind. An open mind says 'yes' rather than 'no'. It considers all things. It opens doors, rather than closing them. Who knows how far you can go? Whether you think you'll fail or succeed, you'll be right.

People often ask me where Heaven is, or, in other words, where the spirit world is. My answer is: it's right here, less than an arm's length away. It exists on a different frequency to our earthly world, and can only be reached when we change our own frequency through meditation and prayer.

Spirit see us from a different angle to how we see ourselves – their view of us is not obscured by worldly concerns or daily moods; it is a much clearer, sharper perception of us. But they still love us, and, while they can't live our lives for us, they can help us understand it better. They have the wisdom and the clarity to help us live our lives as well as we can.

⁓

You can't change the past, and nothing is achieved by dwelling negatively upon it. It's far better to replace your negative thoughts with a positive action in the present.

Fresh air does wonders. If life's feeling overwhelming, step outside and go for a brisk walk to clear your mind.

Love endures no matter what – even when times are tough. Love forgives wrongs and recognises that no one is perfect. Love thinks of others first, and asks for nothing in return.

No one remembers what they have chosen to experience in their lifetime. All you can do is hope that you have chosen well. At the end of the day, if you have chosen to suffer then that's what you will experience, and that will be your path, and I hope you can learn the lessons that you need to grow spiritually.

⁓

If you feel at a loss as to what to do next in your life, look out for signs. Spirit want what's best for you, so sometimes they will leave little clues as to what you should do next. Be patient, and the universe will send you on the right path.

Cherish the time you have with your kids, and make sure you laugh and play with them whenever you can.

Sometimes starting over is the best option. Even though it's hard, don't hold onto something that isn't working if you cannot change it. Learn when to fight for what you want, and when to accept that it's time to move on.

On this earthly plane, it is your job to live, and to let your loved ones go when it is their time. They will always be there when you need them, but in a sense you have to let them move on, too.

I believe in reincarnation. I believe that we are striving to get our angel wings, but that we can only do that by learning as we go, and by becoming a better and better person. This is why we choose the journey we do, as it will always embody the lessons we need to learn in order to progress. We must learn, rather than becoming angry and bitter.

Talk to your loved ones in spirit. Tell them you love them and you miss them. Ask for their help with what's going on with your life. Recall the good times you shared, and pause to give thanks that you had this time together. Let love be the overriding emotion you feel when you remember them, not regret or anger or sorrow. Then accept that they have gone. Acknowledge that you won't see them in the flesh again in this lifetime. But know that you can feel them all around you, that they can come to you in your dreams and that you can talk to them and they will hear you. And that whenever you think about them, they will be right by your side.

People often ask me if we are happy in Heaven. Of course we are, because we no longer carry our load of baggage. We are free to make peace with ourselves and our loved ones, and when we are at peace, we are happy. What a shame we can't achieve enough of that in our earthly lives.

⁓

The baggage that we cart around with us is not always our own. Often we find ourselves worrying about those we love, and sometimes they overburden us with their expectations. This is a particular challenge: how do we remain loving and caring, without accepting a burden that is not ours to carry? Strive to be supportive without taking on another's problems.

Do you sometimes find yourself disappointed in your partner? Perhaps they forgot to do that chore you asked them to help with, or they didn't notice that you were feeling down, or they just never seem to pull their weight with the kids. Communication is key – explain to them what's bothering you, and talk about what you can both do to be there for one another.

When people say they don't know what to do, the answer is, 'Okay, don't do anything. Just wait.' If people learned to wait, they'd find that things would work out the way they had written them before they came into this life.

Take the time to stop and listen to yourself in the midst of your busy life, as you do in meditation. You might detect frustration, irritation, even sadness. This is such a good indication that you are not being true to yourself and your heart. Stop, and let those feelings tell you what is really going on. Those feelings will provide the key to the really big questions about how you actually want to live your life.

Your feelings are very powerful, and it's up to you whether that power works for good or bad in your life. You can create your own prison through feelings and negative thoughts; or you can set yourself free by allowing your feelings to take you to a more positive life.

It might not seem like it at the time, but most steps towards spiritual understanding are taken as a result of facing and dealing with tough times. Your path through life may not always be smooth, but every challenge you face is an opportunity for growth.

Sometimes things happen that we cannot change. Learn from these experiences, and then move on. Dwelling on the past will only bring you heartache.

Spending time with loved ones doesn't have to be an expensive exercise. You could go to the local park for a homemade picnic with your partner, meet a friend for a walk, or take the kids for a day at the beach.

If someone you know has just lost a loved one, write them a card or give them a call to let them know you care and you are there for them if they need anything. Support from friends and family is so important in times of grief.

Sometimes it helps to have something solid to remember someone by. Plant a tree so you can sit under it and recall all the good times you had together, put up a framed photo of them so you think of them each time you walk by, or place a candle somewhere so you can light it whenever you want to take a quiet moment to remember them.

Family is so important. If you haven't spoken to your sibling or parent in a while, reach out and get in touch.

If we could, we would avoid the terrible things that happen to us; but can we grow from them? Can we take awful things and make them into gold? No doubt at all. We are not slaves to the past – unless we choose to be.

When you go into spirit you can be anything you want to be, whatever tickles your fancy. My nan didn't like getting old, so when my nan and pop were reunited they were in their thirties, when they were at their happiest together. How amazing is that?

From the very beginning I felt like a stranger in this world – a foreigner in a small town. I believed then, and now, that my home is in the stars and that one day I'll return there. Don't be scared of going home – I'm looking forward to it. But we are all here until our service is done.

There is a connection of love between the living and the spirit world. I think of it as a rainbow connection or bridge – your friends and family in spirit still care about you and watch over you.

Grieving can't be rushed, so accept that you will need time before normality returns. To help with the healing process, try keeping a diary to record your thoughts and feelings each day.

I believe that before we are born we choose our parents, our family, our friends, the experiences we are going to have in life and also the way we are going to die. Understanding this can help us to be more accepting of all that takes place in our lives.

When you are grieving, pat yourself on the back for every bit of progress you make. It may seem like a small thing to smile again for the first time, or to think of your loved one without feeling angry or bitter, but this is all part of the healing process.

～

We have so many worries nowadays – bills to pay, deadlines to meet, family to care for. But guess what? If you take one day to yourself, away from all that, the world will keep on turning. Nothing is more important than your health and wellbeing.

Love is the most beautiful emotion, and a truly selfless gift you can give to others. To love another and be loved in return is one of life's great joys, but true love does not ask for anything in return.

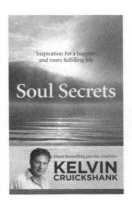

'Don't underestimate the power of positive thoughts. Thinking positively really can change your reality.'

Bestselling psychic medium Kelvin Cruickshank reflects on how to live a full, happy life by making the most of your journey – even in times of loss. Covering key themes of love, grief, forgiveness and belief, Kelvin offers thoughts and affirmations gathered from his own experiences in helping people to connect with spirit. Whether you're seeking reassurance, comfort or motivation to help you on your road through life, you'll find plenty in Kelvin's words to inspire you.

Also by Kelvin Cruickshank

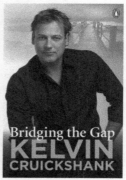

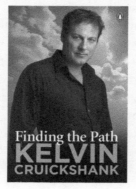

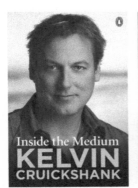

Inside the Medium
KELVIN
CRUICKSHANK

Taking the Journey
KELVIN
CRUICKSHANK

Surrounded by Spirit
KELVIN
CRUICKSHANK